VOLKMAR JOESTEL

MARTIN LUTHER
REBEL AND
REFORMER

A biographical sketch

REFORMATION BIOGRAPHIES
ENGLISH EDITION

DREI KASTANIEN VERLAG

Cover portrait reproduction:
Martin Luther, oil on wood by Lucas Cranach the Elder
(Workshop), 1528

Bibliographic information published by Die Deutsche Bibliothek

Die Deutsche Bibliothek lists this publication in the Deutsche Nationalbiblio-
grafie; detailed bibliographic data are available in the Internet at
http://dnb.ddb.de.

ISBN 3-933028-70-1

© 2003 by DREI KASTANIEN VERLAG

2nd Edition 2004

Drei Kastanien Verlag
Breitscheidstraße 17
Germany – 06886 Lutherstadt Wittenberg

English Translation: Stephen P. Glinsky, Jr.

Pictorial reproductions from originals in the Lutherhalle in Wittenberg:
Wilfried Kirsch Production

Printing: Elbe Printing, Wittenberg GmbH
Printed in Germany

Contents

Prologue: The Secular World and the Church around 1500

On the tenth of November, probably in the year 1483, a son, Martin, was born to the young married couple, Hans Luther, a miner, and his wife, Margarete, as the second of at least nine children. In this hour probably no one suspected what turbulent times were to overtake not only the family, but also the entire society of the Holy Roman Empire of the German Nation, indeed in their ramifications the whole known world, and what an important role their son was to play in Christianity and subsequent European history.

Martin Luther's achievements in his life can only be understood if one takes into account not only his personal development but also the circumstances of his time. An important aspect in the thinking and emotions of an increasing number of people in the late Middle Ages is eloquently testified to by a constantly recurring motif in the art of the time, namely, Christ as the Final Judge (Ill. 1). On the Day of Final Judgment he floats down to the earth on a cloud or a rainbow, to one side of his head a sword, the symbol of eternal damnation, and on the other side a lily, the symbol of grace and of the promise of eternal salvation. Graves open up and those who are just before God are accompanied by angels to the gates of paradise. The wicked are pulled by their hair out of their graves by devils and are thrown into the frightening maw of hell, thus into eternal damnation. Such a mercilessly judgment-rendering Christ was the image the young Luther saw before his eyes in his time in Wittenberg, even literally; the great stone relief can still be viewed in the sacristy of the Wittenberg town church. Similar artistic impressions are manifested in pictorial representations of the Apocalypse, for example, those of Albrecht Dürer, in dance of death portrayals, and astrological predictions of coming catastrophes.

In such ancient fears, rooted in the final analysis in humankind's consciousness of its own mortality, however, also church and religious as well as economic and social events mirrored themselves at the turn of the 15th to the 16th century, which changed the medieval order. One of the social causes was population change. The devastating European

5

Ill. 1 Christ as Final Judge of the World, from Hartmann Schedel: Chronology of the World, Nuremberg, 1493

plague epidemic during the middle of the 14th century wiped out up to a third of the population, above all in the cities. After the middle of the 15th century the population began to grow again, and many young peasants moved to the cities or became day laborers. As a consequence not only individual farms but also entire villages were abandoned. The numbers of those living in the city suburbs swelled, and trade in the outskirts and countryside developed into competition for the traditional city guilds. New natural science knowledge and methods of production led to a boom in mining and metallurgy, in which the provincial princes and rich city dwellers invested their capital, and where many former peasants found a means of living, even if it was hard and entailed much privation. In the end a flight from the countryside ensued, which led to a reduction of agricultural per capita output. Thus on the one hand the feudal pressure on the peasants increased while on the other hand a rise in prices of agricultural products set in. The influx of South American gold into the European economy, as a result of the discovery of America in 1492, reinforced inflationary trends.

There were also new developments in the church. On the one hand the secularization of the clergy, especially at the papal court, continued. The representational needs of the high princes of the church, the financing of both grandiose and expensive Renaissance art projects as well as of wars increased the financial needs of the curia. On the other hand there were counter movements, which to a certain extent prepared the ground for the Reformation. To these belonged the reform movements, which were broadly supported by secular powers, going on since the first half of the fifteenth century, especially in the monastic orders. Above all, harsh or satirical criticism of abuses in the church was voiced from Humanist circles, without calling into question the church's or the pope's roles and power. Here may be mentioned Johann Geiler von Kaisersberg, Sebastian Brant, and the "king of the Humanists", Erasmus of Rotterdam. Amongst the common folk a new longing for divine grace, for eternal salvation, arose. In scholarly research this popular religiosity was also termed the "Sakralisierung" or even "Christianization" of society. Nevertheless the belief in assuring eternal salvation through "good works", which rested on traditional church teaching, led, in part promoted by the church, in part questioned, to an increasing number of pilgrimages, journeys to relic collections and accompanying devotions, mostly connected with donations and offerings

Ill. 2 The Tree of the Estates, woodcut by the Petrarch-Master, ca. 1520

and the gaining of indulgences to take away punishments for sins. Many individuals also believed that by means of stipends and the endowment of masses and yearly remembrances they could "gain" eternal salvation through their own efforts. For the reading of these masses a further increase in the numbers of priests celebrating mass was necessary, who, the longer and the more it went on, were seen as a parasitical social class, since they lived off the income from the masses. Religious brotherhoods arose with a complex mixture of religious and social motivations. Established for the special veneration of a particular saint, they also took over social activities to the extent that they were frequently identified with particular guilds or were at least connected with them, who for their part venerated patron saints.

Social and/or religious movements, whose motives individually can only with difficulty be summed up, increased. A wave of city movements took hold of the land in the 70's through the 90's of the fifteenth century. A renewed intensification took place between 1509 and 1514. Many cities from Constance in the south to Lübeck in the north were caught up in this. Mention should be made in particular of the "crazy year" of 1509 in Erfurt, which Luther himself experienced, but which apparently moved him far less than at times was assumed. Peasant uprisings should also be recalled, such as the "Poor Conrad" movements of 1514 in Württemberg, or those of the Bundschuh in 1493, 1502, and 1513 in southwest Germany.

In 1476 thousands poured into the Franconian town of Niklashausen to hear the anticlerical preaching of "Pfeiferhänslein" (Hans the Piper). After the Flagellant Processions of the fourteenth century sources report sporadically about the persecution of Waldensians in the Thuringia-Saxony region. But whether and to what extent such "heresies" or the ideas, hostile to the church, of the Englishman John Wycliffe and of the Czech reformer Jan Huss helped to prepare for the Reformation, is uncertain.

A new series of university foundings gave notice of an upturn in the sciences: 1456 Greifswald, 1457 Freiburg in Breisgau, 1472 Ingolstadt, 1473 Trier, 1476 Mainz, 1477 Tübingen, 1502 Wittenberg, and 1506 Frankfurt on the Oder. The Wittenberg Leucorea soon developed into the most significant German university. Here the winds of the new age were blowing to the extent that the Humanists and poet laureates (court poets) were put on an equal footing with the academic graduates of the university philosophy departments. In 1518 the grand nephew of the famous Humanist, Johannes Reuchlin, the twenty-one-year old Master Philipp Melanchthon, was to become a professor at the recently established university. In his acceptance speech "On the Necessity of the Improvement of University Instruction" he proclaimed the Humanist education goal and program, with which he established his reputation as "Praeceptor Germaniae" (Teacher of Germany).

In contrast to other European states as, for example, France, England, or Spain, no national monarchy developed. As far as the Habsburger were concerned, it was not a question of national interests, but of the maintenance and consolidation of their universal empire. As a result there was a lack of a strong power at the imperial diets which could have coordinated and brought to fruition the efforts to resolve the German problems which had, for all that, been going on for decades. Consequently the development of a state in Germany took place less in "national" than in territorial state forms.

Childhood and Youth (1483-1505)

Against the background of this tension-laden situation, young Martin grew up. Although he later repeatedly professed being a peasant's son, his father had in the course of years achieved the respected position of a relatively well-off smelting works owner in the prospering Mansfeld copper mining industry. He was, to be sure, from a Thuringian peasant family, but had already migrated to Eisleben prior to Martin's birth. Social processes had thus directly affected the Luther family (Ill. 3).

Shortly after Martin's birth the family moved to Mansfeld, where he attended the Latin School from his fifth to fourteenth year, and there learned, along with writing, singing, and some arithmetic, above all, Latin. The methods of instruction, which strike us today as downright barbaric - canings were the order of the day - left their indelible stamp on the young boy. These experiences were the source of both a more moderate education of his own children as well as of his later reform efforts in schooling. After an interlude at the school of the "Brothers of the Common Life" in Magdeburg in the year 1497, Martin studied at the town pastor's school in Eisenach, where several relatives and acquaintances of the Luther family lived. Particularly the works of classical writers, above all the comedies of the Roman, Publius Terence, left lasting impressions on the young boy.

In the parental home and in school, general folk piety prevailed, to which, it went without saying, belonged the devil and witches. In the home of the Schalbe family in Eisenach the young man learned about the "apocalyptic rapture spirit", Johann Hilten, who had come forward with prophecies critical of the church, in which Luther later became interested. Such experiences were, however, perfectly normal and did not in any way predispose his later development.

The intelligence of his son as well as the hard-won social position of the family, along with its good financial circumstances induced the proud father to let his son, Martin, undertake university studies. In April or May of the year 1501 the young man matriculated at the Erfurt university. After he had earned a baccalaureate in 1502 and a master's degree in 1505 in the philosophy department, he took up the study of law following the wishes of his father, in order to be able to qualify later on for a respected position as a middle class civil servant. But things were to turn out totally differently.

Ill. 3 Luther's Parents, oil on wood by Lucas Cranach the Elder, 1527 (copies made from the originals in the Wartburg)

Monk and Professor of Holy Scripture (1505-1517)

On the return trip to Erfurt from his parents on July 2, 1505, Martin encountered a thunderstorm, and as a result of a terrifying nearby lightning strike he made a vow to become a monk. Why the twenty-two-year-old, full of zest for life, as his former fellow students later reported, made the supposedly sudden decision to enter the cloister, which was incomprehensible for his circle of friends and especially for his disappointed, indeed angered parents, can probably hardly be reconstructed in detail any more. The problem of the accountability of man before God, however, would seem to have played a central role in this matter. "At any rate, the event near Stotternheim, which turned a pious student into a monk, ranks as one of the great and fateful conversions in the history of the church." (Martin Brecht) With his entry into the Erfurt cloister of the Order of Hermits of St. Augustine, with his strict observance of the Order's rules, and with additional penances, the young monk believed he would placate an angry God and thereby assure himself of eternal salvation. Such ideas corresponded completely and in every respect with the system of justification through good works which had been developed over many centuries. The church offered sinners a whole range of penances and purification rituals to free themselves of their sins and justify themselves before God. Above all, the monks considered the strict observance of the vows of poverty, chastity, and obedience, as well as of the Order's rules, as such good works. And these were indeed demanding works. Early at 2 AM the night was over. The so-called canonical hours, the prescribed prayers at certain hours, together with private prayers and readings of holy texts, took place at 3 AM, 6 AM, 9 AM, 12 noon and finally at 3 PM. During the day there were only two meals, of which the first was taken towards noon. In addition there were the yearly periods of fasting. Conscientious monks like Luther fasted even more often and more thoroughly of their own free will. From time to time Martin neither ate nor drank anything for three whole days.

The most important instrument of the church for mediating between human sinfulness and God's forgiveness was confession. This afforded especially the monks the possibility of strict self-examination in order to recognize their sins, to admit them to their father confessor and by means of his words of absolution to perform the works of penance imposed by him. Confession in the cloister was prescribed at least once a week. Again, like many other monks, Martin went to confession even more often. Later he recounted that he once went to confession for six hours. There was an exactly established hierarchy of sins: venial and three grades of mortal sin. For instance, it was considered a venial sin just to laugh or cause others to laugh. Just speaking with a woman was looked upon already as a mortal sin, for which the penance was three days of fasting and a psalm of prayer. Martin, however, became less and less able to distinguish between venial and mortal sins. They all separated him from God. And when could he be sure of having performed enough good works of repentance and penance in order to be justified before God? The monk sank into a hopeless crisis. The more he went to confession and the more penance he performed, the more uncertain he became about whether God really forgave him his sins. Later Luther commented that he had been stuck in monasticism to the point of insanity: "Our hearts were so taken captive by monastic life, that we believed that it alone was the path to blessedness… It is true, I was a devout monk and observed the Order's rules so strictly that I may say: if ever a monk got to heaven through monkery, then I wanted to get there too. All of my cloister companions, who knew me, will testify to that for me. For I would have – if it had lasted longer – martyred myself with keeping vigils, praying, reading, and other tasks… In the end, where is the poor monk with his holiness and purity? He dangles and twists there between heaven and earth, lets himself be praised that he is pure and holy because of his consecration as a monk, and yet his heart and conscience can never experience it." Life in a monk's habit gave him no security. His doubts about it grew visibly.

The central experience in the spiritual life was really holy mass. The consecrated priest changed bread and wine into the body and blood of Christ, and thus to a certain extent reenacted the latter's sacrifice. Here then, in the mass, God was no longer at a great distance or abstract, but here one stood directly before his face and his holiness. This realization then increased, indeed raised to a new level Luther's fear about whether he was worthy of this at all. The idea of standing immediately before the face of an angry God was such an intimidating existential experience for the young monk that he wanted to run away from the altar during his first mass, the Primiz. Although in the end the priest accustomed himself at least outwardly to his task, his dread of the mass remained. And thus even through the priesthood he found no security.

God also led him into the worst trial that a Christian can ever experience, the "Bath of Satan", as the monks called it. Probably in the time between 1515 and 1518 Luther suffered and fought through deep depressions, in which the question martyred him, whether God had not generally and without exception rejected abysmally sinful human beings, so that humans would never be granted God's grace, no matter what they might do. Whoever lives through something like this, experiences it not only as a trial, but also becomes agonizingly aware, that it has to be at the same time the worst sin, namely blasphemy of God. In the end, a single book - holy scripture - brought Luther onto the right and liberating path, even though it was extremely long and stony.

In the summer of 1507 the talented monk was sent by his Order's superiors to study theology at the Erfurt university. Here he studied traditional medieval scholasticism, and also came, however, into contact with Humanistic efforts. In scholasticism there were many schools of thought and systems, which more or less endeavored to combine Christian beliefs with the teachings of classical philosophers, especially of Aristotle, and beyond that to explain and interpret them. In this connection there were opposing viewpoints from the very beginning regarding the "clear" and "pure" text of the Bible, which Luther likewise intensively studied. These tensions were not immediately apparent to him. For that he needed many and diverse stimuli and a long thinking process and experience. Of especially decisive help to him was the methodological criticism of the Humanists, as Helmar Junghans convincingly developed. Their call of "ad fontes" (back to the sources - the foundations of thought of classical antiquity) was gradually applied by Luther to Christianity. Back to the sources meant now for him: back to the word of God, back to holy scripture!

The opportunity and prerequisites for this were afforded the zealous monk by a professorship in biblical studies in

Ill. 4 Christ on the Cross, oil on canvas, Lucas Cranach the Younger, 1571

the theology department of the Wittenberg university. This occurred after he had earned his doctorate in theology in 1512 at the young university, which had been founded only in 1502.

All four of his major lectures from his early period in Wittenberg are preserved. In 1514/15 he lectured on the Psalms, 1515/16 on Paul's Letter to the Romans, 1516/17 on Paul's letter to the Galatians, and finally in 1517/18 on Paul's Letter to the Hebrews. During this time the so-called "reformational discovery" matured in his critical thinking, the realization that sinful humans are justified before God only by his grace, which was visibly mediated by Christ's crucifixion, but never by one's own "good works". Scholarly research is in agreement that this was a rather long process. But it remains disputed whether the decisive change in Luther's thinking took place before or after 1517. According to Luther's own recollection in this connection it was a question of a revelation-like, deeply moving inner experience, which he had during study of Paul's Letter to the Romans in his small study in his Wittenberg monastery tower. Thus also the designation "tower experience". Later the Reformer recalled: "Finally, since I had been thinking about it day and night, I paid attention .... to the connection, namely: the righteousness of God reveals itself in, as is written: The just person lives by faith... At that moment I felt that I had been wholly and completely born again and had entered through the opened gates into paradise itself."

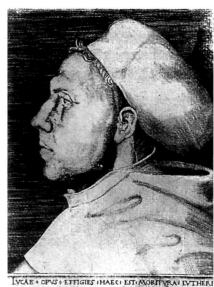

Ill. 5, Luther Wearing Doctor's Cap, copper engraving by Lucas Cranach the Elder, 1521

LVCAE • OPVS • EFFIGIES • HAEC • EST • MORITVRA • LVTHERI
• AETHERNAM • MENTIS • EXPRIMIT • IPSE • SVAE •
• M·D·X·X·I·

Rebel against his Will (1517-1519)

Since about 1514 Luther had not only been a monk and university professor, but also an officially appointed preacher at the Wittenberg city church of St. Mary. Here it was no longer a question of academic theses, pro and contra, but rather the salvation of the "flock". In the sermon, in the hearing of confessions, in administering all the other sacraments as well as the celebration in common of the mass, it was Luther's duty to show people the right way to knowledge of God's will. Here he had to point out clearly the wrong paths, those which led away from God's will. And precisely on this point the pastor collided increasingly with the system of Catholic justification through good works in the form of the dispensation of indulgences.

In the spring of 1517 Luther experienced more and more frequently that the Wittenbergers stayed away from confession and instead streamed over into the towns of Jüterbog and Zerbst, which were situated in Brandenburg or Anhalt territory. This was in order to buy themselves off not only from their penances, but also even from their sins by obtaining indulgences from the charlatan Dominican, Johann Tetzel (Ill. 6). Afterwards they wanted to be absolved by Luther without showing any repentance or improvement. That cut the confessor to the quick, in light of the fact that in an agonizing process he had after all won through to the belief that one had to also and precisely as a sinner love God and therefore demonstrate sorrow and contrition all one's life. Scorning such a view, indulgence preachers now promised that a person could buy oneself free with money from what, in Luther's eyes, was the only possible way to exist as a Christian.

Indulgences had developed over a process of hundreds of years in connection with the sacrament of penance. The sinner had to repent and make this known through confession to a priest, in order to receive absolution from the latter as well as an imposed atonement, that is, a penance. This penance could then be canceled by an indulgence payment. The old concept behind this was that the church had amassed a limitless "church treasury" through the sufferings of Christ and the saints, which the bishops and priests could then distribute to sinners.

Ill. 6 Caricature of Tetzel's Sale of Indulgences, woodcut, 1617

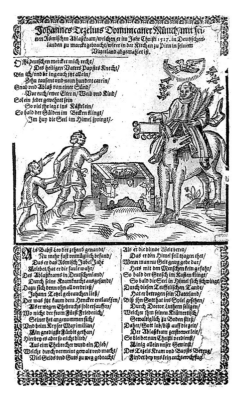

As a result of late medieval socio-economic processes the practice of indulgences degenerated finally into inscrutable financial and political transactions. In the course of enormous growth in the financial requirements of the curia, the latter distributed these indulgence letters to church institutions with the right to sell indulgences for penances. Frequently the sale of indulgences was tied to the display of relic collections, which had likewise come into fashion. The second-largest collection in Christianity had been gotten together at the Wittenberg All Saints' Foundation by the pious Elector Frederick the Wise. The oldest relic and showpiece of this collection was a purported thorn from Christ's crown of thorns. Even though Luther had looked with mistrust upon this indulgence as well as all the others even before the publication of his theses, it wasn't this one which precipitated his rebellion. Rather it was the so-called St. Peter's indulgence, which Pope Julius II had proclaimed, in order to complete the new construction of St. Peter's Basilica in Rome, which had begun in 1505. In 1515 Pope Leo X assigned the sale of this indulgence in Germany to the Hohenzollern Prince and Cardinal Albert. The cardinal, however, had become the bishop of Magdeburg and administrator of the diocese of Halberstadt in 1513 and even the archbishop of Mainz in 1515. For this accumulation of benefices, which was actually illegal, he had to pay money in the amount of 29,000 gulden to the curia in Rome. In addition he had to take out a loan from the rich Fugger family in Augsburg. From the indulgence monies, which were to be taken in, one half was to be transferred to Rome for the construction of St. Peter's, while the cardinal was to be allowed to keep the other half, over 36,000 gulden, in order to pay off his debt to the Fuggers. Albrecht then had his vice-commissioners draw up a set of instructions. On the basis of these instructions the notorious Dominican, Johann Tetzel, went into the Magdeburg and Brandenburg regions north of Wittenberg, traveling through the towns and villages and offering indulgences for sale, like a market hawker. Soon there were rumors, certainly exaggerated, going around everywhere about him. It was said that a person could even obtain indulgences from Tetzel for the sins of people already dead. And who could bear to let recently deceased relatives or acquaintances roast in purgatory, if one could open the way to paradise for them by paying a certain sum? It was also said that Tetzel sold indulgences for sins one would only commit in the future. Wasn't that the best life insurance a person could imagine for oneself? Indeed, it was even said, blasphemously, that Tetzel could also, if this were possible, forgive the mortal sin of raping the mother of God, through an indulgence. But it must be expressly emphasized that it wasn't these obvious, "Christian" motivated financial manipulations which aroused Luther's anger. Humanist-influenced irony and satire, witticisms, spoken off the record or even openly, were definitely not a seldom thing. Erasmus of Rotterdam, for example, said maliciously, if one were to gather together all of the alleged splinters of Christ's cross which were revered as relics, there would be enough wood for a fleet of ships. No. Luther's motives were different: with such a view of indulgences as Tetzel spread about, Luther's conviction was actually ridiculed, namely, that sinful human beings had to submit themselves their whole lives long to God's majesty contritely and in humility. With the indulgence practices, however, a comfortable, superficial, and therefore false path was promised to the faithful, which was insulting to God's majesty. This had to be stopped. On occasion already Luther had spoken out against the abuse of indulgences. Above all in sermons he had repeatedly impressed upon his listeners that God's honor is diminished when one acquires indulgences without true repentance and penance. But now it was time to have recourse to responsible authorities, in order to bring about the withdrawal of the indulgence instructions and the cessation of the shameful actions of the indulgence preacher. On October 31, 1517 Luther wrote letters to his ecclesiastical superiors, bishop Hieronymus Schulze of Brandenburg and archbishop Albert of Magdeburg. Possibly he also wrote to still other bishops. Only the letter to Albert is still preserved. Obviously written "in fear and trembling and with prayer" (Martin Brecht), it at least conveys the impression that Luther was well aware of the volatility of the problem addressed. If he presented himself as a true advocate of the interests of the bishop and the pope, that certainly was not due to calculated tactics, but resulted from the earnest hope that both of them might put an end to the indulgence abuse practices. Luther had then included 95 theses in this letter to Cardinal Albert. They pose penetrating and critical questions regarding the prevailing practice of selling indulgences, without questioning indulgences as a whole or by no means the church and its representatives as mediators of salvation. Nevertheless it was definitely no accident, as occasionally can be read, that it was precisely the indulgence dispute which led to the conflict with Rome. In contrast, the theses which were published shortly before the 95 indulgence theses were actually theologically more significant against scholastic theology. The 95 indulgence theses, although unintentionally and unexpectedly, were nevertheless and for those reasons all the more effective, since they aimed directly at the core of the church's presumptuous power over the conscience of the people.

Even to the present day it has practically been part of the educational canon that Martin Luther nailed these 95 theses on the door of the castle church in Wittenberg on October 31, 1517 (Ill. 7), in order to hold a disputation on them. Es-

Ill. 7 Castle Church in Wittenberg, woodcut by Lucas Cranach the Elder, 1509

pecially in the 19th century this event inspired the imagination of artists.

In 1961, however, the Catholic Luther scholar, Erwin Iserloh, made public the sensational claim that the nailing up of these theses belonged to the world of legend. This amounted to a sensation, since this event had after all been celebrated for centuries as the symbol of Protestantism. The vehement discussion it provoked has not been in a position, even up today, to settle the problem conclusively.

On the other hand it is established, with or without a nailing up of the theses, that a public disputation on these theses did not take place either in Wittenberg or any other place. At first nothing at all happened. Reactions failed to appear, both in Wittenberg and from friends to whom Luther had sent the theses, as well as from the bishop.

Notwithstanding that, Luther obviously found himself in a state of liberated high spirits after sending off the theses. From the beginning of November, 1517 he often signed his letters with "Eleutherius" . That is a Greek-Latin word construct (Greek: eleutheros = free). Luther looked upon himself therefore as "the free man" or "the freed man" . In this the feeling is probably expressed that he had now crossed his "Rubicon", naturally not in the sense of a break with the church, but more likely from the knowledge of having drawn practical consequences from insights gained. It becomes clear that Luther was aware of the explosiveness of the theme for church practice, that he had broken into a wasps' nest.

Apart from the bishops Luther had sent the theses to only a very few close friends. Nonetheless, in so doing he had unleashed a chain reaction. Through copies the theses reached, among others, Nuremberg, Leipzig, and Basel, where they were printed by December 1517 or early 1518. From this point in time on it was true what Luther himself later put into words, the theses "ran through all of Germany in only 14 days" .

The reactions of the bishops were at first quite different. The Merseburg bishop was to a great extent dependent on Duke George of Saxony. The latter on the other hand, as a protagonist of far-reaching church reform, was initially very much in agreement with Luther's stepping forward against indulgences. The Brandenburg bishop Schulze kept a low profile, advised, however, against pursuing the matter any further. The most powerful and influential cleric, archbishop Albert, first requested an expert opinion from the Mainz university, informed the pope immediately, and demanded of the Magdeburg councilors, that they forbid Luther any further hindrance of the indulgence preacher. The Mainzer opinion of December 17th refrained from a judgment of its own, but recommended an investigation of the matter by the Roman curia. The latter did not see itself at all constrained to drastic action. On February 3, 1518 Pope Leo X merely pointed out to the Vicar General of the Hermits of St. Augustine that he should influence Luther in the direction of restraint. Tetzel, who felt personally hurt, is supposed to have burst out with death threats against Luther in his anger, but afterward reacted first on the academic level too. On January 20, 1518 he took part in a disputation at the Frankfurt on the Oder university on a series of theses on indulgences. When booksellers appeared with printed copies of these theses in Wittenberg, students took all 800 copies from them and burned them by way of a demonstration.

We know very little regarding Luther's own attitude after the sending of his theses, his hopes and his fears. The first known comment does not come until February 15, 1518. He convincingly described here his shock that the theses, in which he after all had been concerned about nothing except the salvation of the souls of Christians, had vaulted so quickly into the sphere of higher politics. He had been suspected of being nothing more than a lackey of the Elector of Saxony. The Elector had namely forbidden the selling of the St. Peter's indulgence in his Saxon territories even before the nailing up of the theses. The Elector's competitor, the archbishop of Magdeburg, was not to be allowed to increase his economic power with, of all things, good Saxon money. The accusation of opportunism, which is even today occasionally made against Luther, is incorrect, even though it goes without saying that religious, economic, social, and political relationships and interests were bound up precisely with the indulgence question.

Even prior to a planned, comprehensive commentary on his theses there appeared in print in April 1518 a sermon given in the second half of March. Under the title "A Sermon on Indulgences and Grace" Luther set forth in a concise and understandable form, and what was most especially important, in the German language, his by now unquestionably personal view of the indulgence dispute. This paper became his first major literary success. Prior to 1520 alone a total of 20 printings appeared in Wittenberg, Leipzig, Nuremberg, Augsburg, and Breslau. Here the special role of the new book-printing technology in the spread of new ideas became vividly clear. It was, to use the modern expression, just once, a media revolution.

Now events began to develop faster and faster. The inability of the curia even just to see Luther's justified religious concerns led to repression instead of discussion. And the heavier this became, the more he was really forced to express his views in concrete terms and defend them. As early as March 1518 the noted Ingolstadt theology professor, Johann Eck, who up till then was definitely sympathetic to his Wittenberg colleague, characterized the rebellious one for the first time as a Bohemian (alluding to the "heretical" Hussites), and a heretic. Taking his cue from this, Tetzel published a tract end of April, beginning May 1518 in which he portrayed Luther as a heretic in the tradition of Wycliffe and

Huss. Luther's printed answers to these rebukes now also became polemic. In this conflict all of the later controversial issues were laid out in initial formulations, such as the power of free will, the sacraments, the pope's authority to dispense absolution, and the priestly fullness of power. It presaged a fundamental authority conflict, even though Luther still cherished the hope the pope would defend him. In the summer of 1518, however, heresy proceedings in Rome were officially instituted against him.

The various conflicts and differing interests gave way for a short time to the alternatives: for Luther or against Luther. The spontaneous reform movement ushered in by the theses pushed their author farther and farther, at first against his own will, in his struggle against Rome. One stage on this path was the "fatherly examination" of Luther by Cardinal Cajetan on the occasion of the Augustinian Assembly in October of 1518 in Augsburg (Ill. 8), after Elector Frederick refused to extradite the rebellious monk to Rome. Luther himself spoke of it as the most difficult passage of his life, with after all the fate of Jan Huss, i.e., being burned at the stake, before his eyes. But he was not prepared to recant. He escaped threatened arrest by fleeing Augsburg during the night of October 20 to 21 .

Ill. 8 Luther before Cardinal Cajetan, colored woodcut, 1557

After the death of Emperor Maximilian at the beginning of 1519, outrageous bargaining over his successor ensued. With the help of the Fugger, Charles I of Spain was able to raise the highest bribe monies for the Electors, thus routing his rivals Francis I of France and Henry VIII of England from the field, and on June 28, 1519 was elected Emperor as Charles V. In deference to the vote of the powerful Elector Frederick of Saxony, the heresy proceedings against Luther were suspended, especially in view of the fact that the papal chamberlain, Karl von Miltitz, had worked out an agreement at the beginning of June, whereby neither side would engage in polemics. This state of affairs gave the reform movement a respite and thus the possibility of consolidating and expanding.

A conflict of opinion which had originated from Luther's indulgence theses was argued in a public disputation between the Ingolstadt theologian Johann Eck and Luther's fellow disputant Andreas Bodenstein, called Karlstadt. This took place in the Leipzig Pleißenburg from June 27 to July 14, 1519 and dealt at first with the absolutely central theme of the relationship between human will and divine grace. When the disputation between Karlstadt and Eck reached an impasse, Luther stepped into the fray (Ill.9).

Ill. 9 Leipzig Disputation in 1519, colored woodcut, 1557

From the very beginning on Eck's intention was to expose Luther as a heretic. In the argument regarding the authority of the pope and of the councils, Luther contested the divine origin of the papacy, declaring that among the views of Jan Huss were those that were perfectly properly Christian, and that even councils can err, indeed had erred. At this point Eck believed he could triumph. He declared Luther a heretic, with which however he only achieved that the popularity of the Wittenberg monk became even greater. Especially scholars coming from Humanist circles seized enthusiastically upon Luther's ideas. However, Duke George the Bearded of Saxony, was from that moment on an embittered foe of the Reformation. The background of this fateful anti-Reformation commitment of the Duke was complex. In addition to the political competition with his cousin, Elector Frederick, an important factor was the knowledge, which burdened George his whole life, that he was a grandson of the Bohemian "Heretic King" Georg Podiebrad, who was excommunicated by the Roman church. Thus, for all his desire for reform, he decisively rejected any initiative which showed even initial signs of being anti-Rome and "heretical".

Flight from Excommunication and the Imperial Ban (1520-1521)

The years 1520 and 1521 were decisive years for the reform movement. Martin Luther was now developing his religious thoughts into an independent theology and working out a broad program of church and secular reforms, through which he inwardly finally separated himself from Rome. This separation found its external reflection in the imposition of the papal excommunication on the Reformer as well as in his fearless defense of his teachings before the Diet of Worms.

In 1520 Luther basically undertook a fundamental criticism of the teachings of the Roman church in three reformational writings and developed a comprehensive reform program.

The first and in its time most popular tract appeared on August 12, 1520 and was directed *To the Christian Nobility.*

Luther refuted the teachings of the church that religious power was above secular power and that only the pope might interpret the bible and summon a council: "With great skill the Romanists have erected three walls around themselves, with which they have protected themselves up till now, so that no one has been able to reform them. As a result, the whole of Christendom has fallen dreadfully. First, when put under pressure, they said that temporal power had no authority over them, but that on the contrary, spiritual power was above the temporal. Second, when an effort was made to criticize them based on holy scripture, they contended that no one had the right to interpret scripture except the pope. Third, if they were threatened with a council, they invented the fiction that no one could summon a council except the pope... May God help us and give us one of the trumpets with which the walls of Jericho were thrown down, so that we can also topple these walls made of straw and paper, and to unloose the Christians rods, which are for punishment, to bring to light the cunning and deceitfulness of the devil for the purpose of mending our ways through punishment and again earning his favor. . . "

AETHERNA IPSE SVAE MENTIS SIMVLACHRA LVTHERV EXPRIMIT AT VVLTVS CERA LVCAE OCCIDVOS

· M·D·X·X·

Ill. 10 Luther as a Monk, copper engraving by Lucas Cranach the Elder, 1520

Through baptism every believer is himself priest, bishop, and pope. This teaching of the priesthood of all the believers meant the rejection of the mediator function of the priestly hierarchy between God and man. Basing himself upon this teaching, Luther demanded the secularization of church possessions, the dissolution of all orders, and pastors' eligibility for election by the congregations. As the only legitimate hierarchy he acknowledged the secular authorities, whom he called upon to step to the head of the reform movement and to carry out reforms on the national level.

With his tract *On the Babylonian Captivity of the Church*, first published in Latin in the first days of October in the year 1520, Luther attacked the core of the old church teaching, the doctrine of the sacraments. In place of the seven old sacraments he accepted only one true one, the word of God, and three sacramental signs (baptism, penance and the Lord's supper). All other sacraments of the old church (confirmation, holy orders, marriage, and extreme unction) were rejected by Luther as the work of man. And with this too he dealt a severe blow to the exclusivity of the priestly class.

In *On the Freedom of a Christian Person,* completed in only two days, Luther decisively rejected the Roman papal teaching infallibility in doctrinal questions by means of the following paradox that is remarkable even today: "So that we can really know what a Christian is, and what the meaning of the freedom is, which Christ has merited for him and given him … I wish to put to put forward these two conclusions: a Christian is a sovereign master over all things and not subservient to anyone. A Christian is a menial servant in all things and subservient to everyone." The new ideal of piety was directed both against the papacy as well as against a "carnal", that is, secular interpretation of the gospel. This tract represented, even though in a spiritualized form, a further attack on the foundations of the Roman church, since Luther gave expression to the fact that there was only one binding authority for Christians in questions of faith: the word of God.

The papal chamberlain, Karl von Miltitz, once again tried in a conversation with the Reformer on October 11, 1520, to induce him to make concessions and to reconcile himself with the pope. Afterward Luther wrote a letter to Pope Leo X, wherein he expressed complete respect and reverence for him personally, however did not withdraw any point of his attacks against the papacy as an institution. He enclosed the freedom tract in this letter.

At the beginning of the year 1520 the heresy proceedings against the refractory monk had been taken up again. It reached a high point first of all on June 15, 1520 with the publication of the bull threatening excommunication, *Exsurge Domine* (Rise up, O Lord),which had for the most part been drawn up by Prierias, Cajetan, and Eck. This bull granted the rebel a period of 60 days within which to recant his teachings and demanded the burning of his books. On the basis of papal authority Eck in addition threatened Luther's collaborators Karlstadt and Johann Dölsch von Feldkirchen, the Zwickauer Egranus, the Nuremberger Humanist Pirckheimer as well as the town clerk there, Spengler, with excommunication. On July 17 Eck and Aleander were authorized as nuncios to publish, disseminate and execute the bull. Eck was sent to Saxony, Aleander to the Netherlands. Eck had hardly any success. For the most part the bull was reacted to with disregard or open scorn and ridicule. Aleander's mission was at first more successful. On October 8 and 15 he had Lutheran books solemnly burned in Louvain and Liège. After he once again succeeded in this in Cologne on November 12, a similar action failed in Mainz on November 29; Luther's followers burned writings from his opponents in place of Luther's.

As the news of the threatened excommunication spread, spontaneous demonstrations supporting the Reformer took place in many towns. Students and university lecturers at the Erfurt university stood up publicly for their former colleague. Aroused Franconian nobles, such as Franz von Sickingen and Silvester von Schaumburg, offered Luther military protection.

Luther decided upon a demonstrative step. A poster called upon the Wittenberg students to gather on December 10 at 9 AM in front of the Elster Gate not far from the Holy Cross hospital. Surrounded by jubilation and applause, the Reformer threw into the flames church law books, writings of Eck, Emser, and other opponents, and finally a copy of the bull threatening excommunication, and precisely at the place where otherwise vagabonds who had died from epidemics were burned. While doing so he is supposed to have called out, "Because you, godless book, have afflicted or brought dishonor upon the holy ones of the Lord, may in

the same way eternal fire afflict and consume you." (Ill. 11)

This sensational act of the Reformer signified his final and irrevocable separation from Rome, as he himself emphasized on the next day in his lecture. Subsequently, on January 3, 1521, the pope proclaimed the excommunication of Luther with the bull *Decet Romanum pontificem,* which of course produced hardly any noticeable effect. According to existing law the Emperor now would have had to declare immediately the imperial ban. At the imperial diet, however, which was convened at Worms on January 27, 1521, many imperial estates insisted that Luther not be condemned without being heard, and that he be summoned before the imperial diet for an examination. Some princes saw in the Reformation, in addition to their individual, mostly probably honest religious decisions, the possibility of diminishing Rome's influence in German politics and thus of expanding political power in their own territories as well as acquiring administrative power over church possessions and incomes. These forces succeeded and Luther was officially invited before the imperial diet on March 6, 1521. He was assured protective escort. On April 2 the Reformer set out. His traveling companions were, among others, his friend Nikolaus von Amsdorf as well as the imperial herald Kaspar Sturm. The trip resembled a triumphal procession. Everywhere the

Reformer was enthusiastically greeted and called upon to preach. In spite of the danger threatening, his courage was undaunted. He is supposed to have said, "Even if there were as many devils in Worms as tiles on the roofs, I would still want to go to the city!" . The wave of enthusiasm and his consciousness of acting as the instrument of God gave Luther the strength, as an insignificant monk, to go before the mightiest of the Holy Roman Empire and to defend his teaching. On April 16 Luther and his company reached Worms. On the afternoon of April 17 Luther was ordered before the imperial diet and called upon by the imperial ecclesiastical official, Johann von der Ecken, to recant his teaching. Following the recommendations of the Saxon electoral councilors, he requested a day of deliberation. On April 18 it was suggested to Luther that he recant at least a part of his writings. Thereupon the Reformer divided these into polemic writings against the papacy, argumentative writings against opponents, and edifying pieces. In his polemic writings he admitted, to be sure, that he had been more impetuous than was proper for a monk. But he categorically refused to recant any of his teachings. He concluded his address with the words: "Unless I am proven wrong by the testimony of scripture or by correct reasoning; for I do not believe in either the pope or the councils alone, since it is clear as day that they have erred several times and contradicted themselves… I am convinced by the scriptures I have presented, and my conscience is bound to the word of God. Therefore I neither can nor want to retract anything, because to act against one's conscience is difficult, harmful, and dangerous. God help me, amen." The famous words: "Here I stand, I cannot do otherwise." are a later embellishment.

With this none the less courageous stand, Luther gave the reform movement a powerful moral boost. In Worms an indescribable excitement reigned. A poster was put up with the blunt threat that 400 knights also stood ready to take military action on behalf of Luther and the Reformation. A flood of leaflets and flyers about his appearance before the Emperor and the empire spread through the entire land and heralded everywhere the courageous act of the Wittenberg monk. The young Emperor, however, whom Luther had described as late as 1520 with high hopes as a "noble young man", was from this hour on an embittered opponent of

Ill. 12 Luther before the Imperial Diet of Worms, colored woodcut, 1557

Luther, and he swore to himself he would fight the heresy with every means and destroy it root and branch.

After further, nevertheless futile efforts to change Luther's mind, he received the order to leave Worms on April 25, 1521. Only after he himself and his companions, as well as a good part above all of the princes and dignitaries supporting the Reformer had already left Worms, did the Emperor, with the consent of the remaining diet members, decree the imperial ban of the Reformer on May 26, 1521. However, he had it back-dated to May 8 so as to create the impression that the entire imperial diet had agreed to it. The ban required of everyone, neither to give shelter to the condemned person nor to spread his teachings, to capture and hand him over to the imperial authorities, as well as to neither read his books nor to buy or sell them.

From Word to Deed (1521-1525)

On the return journey from the Imperial Diet at Worms the Reformer was "abducted" on the evening of May 4, 1521 and taken to the Wartburg by servants of the Elector. Only a few with inside information knew of this. A rumor even circulated that Luther had been murdered. The famous Albrecht Dürer in Nuremberg lamented, "O God, if Luther is dead, who will expound to us so clearly the holy gospel? O God, what would he have been able to write for us in the next 10 or 20 years? O, all of you devout Christians, help me shed copious tears for this divinely inspired man."

With his "disappearance" the dangers threatening both himself and also the Elector were to be minimized. For excommunication and the imperial ban endangered all who were guilty of protecting heretics and banned persons. By removing Luther from the immediate arguments, the Elector assured the Reformation as a whole of favorable conditions for development. It was a distinctive example of the both spirited and well-thought-out politics of the "Saxon fox", as people, both enviously and respectfully, called Frederick the Wise (Ill. 13).

In seclusion from the loud goings-on of the world, "in the solitude", up on "Patmos", "in the kingdom of the birds", as Luther himself wrote, he suffered again in the Wartburg

Ill. 13 Elector Frederick the Wise, oil on wood by Lucas Cranach the Elder (Workshop), 1532

from increasing physical difficulties and trials in the form of pestering from the devil, whereby it must be kept in mind that the alleged throwing of the inkwell is a later legend. Letter writing to Wittenberg and an absolutely enormous work-load nevertheless distracted "Squire George" from his difficulties.

Luther composed interpretations of the Magnificat and of several psalms. In June he refuted a critical study by the Catholic theologian, Latomus, at the same time further developing his justification teaching. In addition he wrote against a condemnation document of the Paris university and against the efforts of Cardinal Albert to proclaim a new indulgence in Halle. The latter writing, *Against the New Idol in Halle,* caused temporary disagreements with Spalatin, the Elector's secretary, since the secretary, out of fear of new complications, refused its printing in Wittenberg.

Since Luther's preaching activity was suspended, he then set to work composing model sermons for the entire church year, The German Postil. The Christmas and Advent section was completed in the Wartburg. Later Luther characterized it as his best book.

But the translation of the New Testament from the origi-

Ill. 14 Luther Translating the Bible (after Dürer's "St. Jerome"), copper engraving by Wolfgang Stuber, ca. 1580

nal Greek into German was the most important and momentous work. The Reformer accomplished this enormous task in only 10 weeks (Ill. 14). Printed in Wittenberg from July to September 1522, it began its triumphal procession around the world as the *September Testament*. Regarding its effectiveness the Luther opponent, Cochläus, later wrote, "Before, however, Emser's work (a Catholic bible translation - Volkmar Joestel) saw daylight, Luther's New Testament was reproduced by the printer to such an extent and disseminated in such large numbers, that even tailors and shoemakers, indeed also women and other simple folk, so many accepted this new Lutheran gospel, who had only learned to read some little German (from sayings) on a gingerbread cookie. They read this (gospel) with the greatest eagerness, as if it were a fountain of all truth. Some carried it around in their bosoms and learned it by heart."

In the meantime Luther's fellow protagonists in Wittenberg began with practical reforms, at first completely in agreement with and with encouragement by letter from "Squire George" . In the middle of December 1521 he wrote to Spalatin, "Should there be perhaps only unceasing disputation over the word of God and should the deed never come to fruition?" Already in May 1521 three priests in different regions had by way of demonstration gotten married. The Wittenberg Augustinians, impelled by the fiery sermons of the monk, Gabriel Zwilling, reformed first the monastery's divine service, and in the end dissolved in effect the Saxon congregation in a chapter meeting in January 1522. In Wittenberg, on the one hand, university professors, under the leadership of Andreas Bodenstein, and on the other hand of the city council, set about reforming both the divine services as well as the social life of the town. The carrying out of the accepted new town order was, however, forbidden by the court. The Elector saw in it an impermissible encroachment on his jurisdiction.

Luther himself observed the reforms with great interest and even supported them through publications. In letters he wrote against priestly celibacy. In two significant writings, completed in November 1521, he repudiated monks' vows and demanded reform of the divine services. When, however, more radical forces under the influence of the "Zwickau prophets", who had come to Wittenberg, began to stage in part violent actions, threatened priests, and tried to coerce people into the new beliefs, Luther turned decisively against such a "carnal" interpretation of the bible. After a short visit in the Elbe town in December 1521, he composed a writing on this subject, *A Sincere Admonition to All Christians to Guard Against Insurrection*. In addition to the appeal to his followers, only to engage themselves with the word, but not with violence for the Reformation, Luther assessed in this writing also his own work: "What is Luther? After all, the teaching is not mine. Nor was I crucified for anyone. St. Paul would not permit Christians to call themselves Pauline or Petrine, but Christian. How then should I – poor, stinking sack of maggots that I am – be entitled to have people call the children of Christ by my wretched name?"

After the first significant "iconoclastic attack" in the Reformation period on February 6, 1522, which was sanctioned by a council resolution, nothing more held back the worried Reformer on his "Patmos". Having arrived back in Wittenberg on March 6, he gave his famous Lenten Sermons for a week long starting on March 9. With these he steered the movement back into moderation. Most of the innovations he revoked. The "adiaphora", things that God had neither commanded nor forbidden, were permitted again by Luther. To these belonged fasting and images in churches. In deference to those "weak in their faith" Luther, however, also permitted for a time things that were actually not evangelical, such as a form of the Lord's supper and saints' feasts. "Summing up then, I want to preach, I want to speak out, I want to write, but I don't want to coerce or constrain anyone with violence, for faith needs to be willing and not compelled and to be accepted freely."

From this time on the more radical heads had either to submit themselves (Gabriel Zwilling) or they were forbidden to publish and in the end left town (Andreas Bodenstein).

Luther's position to be sure was derived first and foremost from his fundamental religious convictions, but over and above that also reflected the real political and confessional factions in the empire. In the Nuremberg imperial government especially Duke George of Saxony pressed for an uncompromising fight against the Reformation. The clever tactics of the electoral Saxon ambassadors in the government nevertheless prevented harsh mandates. The Second

Nuremberg Imperial Diet in 1522/23 finally declared the carrying out of the excommunication and imperial ban to be impossible, and demanded instead a free German National Council. Until then the parties in conflict should not engage in public polemics. That meant on the whole a notable success for the Reformation and assured it the possibility of further consolidation and expansion. To be sure, the Third Nuremberg Imperial Diet in 1524 demanded again compliance with the Edict of Worms. But now the position of the evangelicals was already well enough secured, that a forcible carrying out of this decree seemed to be no longer feasible to the Catholic believers.

Against this background Luther began to formulate the basic concepts of his political ethics. It was first a matter of the problem of possible resistance by the (evangelical) princes against the (Catholic) Emperor, and later also of the fundamental right of subjects to resist secular authorities. On the 24th and 25th of October 1522 the Reformer preached in Weimar before Duke John. These sermons appeared in print in December under the title *On Secular Authorities, To What Extent People Owe Them Obedience*. It remained Luther's fundamental work on his political ethics and formulated the teaching of the "two governments" of God. For the faithful it was the word, for those without faith it was the sword of secular authority. Since the majority of mankind was not under the governance of Christ, but of the devil, secular authority was required, whose duty it was to govern according to reason and love of neighbor. To want to govern the world, which fundamentally belongs to the devil, according to the gospel, would lead to chaos. In the first part Luther postulated the fundamental necessity of all Christians submitting to the secular authorities. In the second part he described in clear terms the latter's limits. Secular laws may only be applied to the body and earthly goods, but never to souls and faith. Faith was exclusively a matter of conscience and was not under any secular control. Luther also warned authorities that the people, gradually becoming wise, would not put up with their arbitrariness in the long run: "For there are only very few princes whom people don't consider to be fools or scoundrels. That comes from the fact that they also act as such. And the common person is beginning to understand, and the punishment for the princes, which God calls 'contempt', is gaining power among the people and the common person... people will not, people can not, people don't want to suffer your tyranny and your wantonness for long." On the other hand a Christian must not requite this arbitrariness with the same thing, "For one should not resist the authorities with violence, but only by acknowledgment of the truth. If they respect this, it is good, if not, you are not to blame and suffer injustice for the sake of God." Referring to Reformation teaching, the Franconian knight Franz von Sickingen attempted in 1522/23 to prevent the downfall of lesser nobility with military action against the Elector of Trier. In a counter-attack of the Swabian Bund and of the princes, Sickingen was defeated, many knights' castles destroyed, and the political independence of the lesser nobility largely broken. Luther followed Sickingen's actions with definite sympathy and was disconcerted over the failure and death of the knight. Yet he had never left any doubt that he rejected the knights' uprising as "rebellion". Thus he prevented the Reformation being drawn into this relatively peripheral but for all that dangerous social conflict regarding knighthood.

In order to give the word of God more and more exposure, the Reformer accelerated his preaching activity (Ill. 15). In April and May of 1522 sermon trips brought him to Borna, Altenburg, Zwickau, Eilenburg, Torgau, and Zerbst, in autumn to Erfurt and Weimar. In the following year he gave a total of 137 sermons. Despite all the variations his self-determined theme remained the same: "Believe in God, help your neighbor, that is what the whole gospel teaches." In 1524 he warned: "I believe that Germany has never before heard as much of God's word as it has now... Dear Germans, buy, as long as the market is in front of your door, reap the harvest, as long as there is sunshine and good weather, make use of God's grace and word, as long as they are here! For you should know this: God's word and grace is a passing cloudburst, which does not come back again to where it once was... Rome and the Latin land have also had it; but gone is gone, now they have the pope. And you Germans must not think that you will have it forever. For ingratitude and contempt will not enable it to stay here. Therefore take hold of it and hang onto it tightly, whoever can do so! Lazy hands are bound to have a bad year."

Finally Luther reached the conclusion that God's word had now become so powerful, that the deference in respect

Ill. 15   Luther Preaching, woodcut 1588

to the "weak ones", which was the basis of restraining reforms, could no longer be justified. The church and political reform demands of many classes of society at the Altenburg provincial diet in the spring of 1523 underscored
this view. Luther was also confirmed in his resolve by the
visible success of the Reformation in other territories, such
as Switzerland, significant south German cities and in the, at
that time, political, cultural, and economic center of Nuremberg.

   Preparatory to the actual reforms were, among others,
two writings published already in 1522, which were to become "best sellers", the Personal Prayer Book and the German Baptismal Book. In January of 1523 Luther became serious. Whoever still took offense now at the reforms, was
not weak, but stubborn. In clear terms he summed it up:
"Three great abuses have occurred in the divine service.
The first, that God's word is hidden... that is the worst
abuse. The second, since God's word has been hidden, so
many un-Christian fables and lies have come beside it... The
third, since people have performed such a divine service as
a work, in order to obtain God's grace and blessedness,
faith has gone under." Luther demanded the binding introduction of the Lord's supper in both forms. In the writing,

On the Order of Public Worship, he justified the reform. The crucial points were to be, at least for priests, pastors, and school children, a daily early divine service with an Old Testament lesson, sermon, prayer, psalm, and antiphonal songs, as well as a daily afternoon divine service given over to the reading and interpretation of the New Testament. The Sunday congregational divine service was kept for the time being as a purified divine service mass with traditional church hymns. Most of the festivals of the saints were either done away with or were transferred to the following Sunday. On March 11, 1523 the Reformer declared the daily endowed private masses to be terminated. Finally, On December 4, 1523 the *Formula Missae* (Form of the Mass) appeared in print. With this the Lutheran divine service order was presented in completed form. For the rest it left many things optional, such as the elevation (raising) of the host and the chalice, the use of priestly mass vestments, confession, and fasting and prayers before receiving the sacrament. The "canon" however, with which a sacrifice had been made out of the mass, disappeared without any replacement. The Lord's supper in both forms was made binding. Although since October 9, 1524 Luther himself had no longer ascended the pulpit in a monk's habit, but in secular scholarly garb, a long black cloak, he allowed continued use of the old, ornate mass vestments. Only after the intervening period up to 1548 did the orthodox Lutherans endeavor to establish finally the long, black cloak and the biretta, the "Luther gown", as the uniform garb of preachers.

Whether Luther in his divine service reform allowed himself to be inspired by similar contemporary activities, for example, Thomas Müntzer's in Allstedt, is disputed in research. What is established, is that Luther's reforms, seen in the consistency of his thought and actions, lay in this time.

It goes without saying that German hymns also belong to the evangelical divine service. At the end of 1523 the Reformer informed Spalatin of his decision to compose German psalms and sacred songs for the people, and called upon the electoral secretary and other co-workers to do the same thing. Individual parts of the liturgy were to be sung in German by the entire congregation. Already in 1523 Luther's first song texts appeared in individual printings, and finally in 1524 in Nuremberg the *Achtliederbuch* was printed with four hymn texts by Luther as well as additional collections. The most significant early collection, containing 24 of Luther's hymns, was the choir hymn book by Johann Walter, the electoral composer and conductor. The fact that Luther himself also composed can be authenticated only for the hymn "A Mighty Fortress is Our God", which of course did not originate until later.

The divine service reform encountered vehement resistance in Wittenberg from the All Saints Foundation. Even in 1521 Luther had called it a "Bethaven", that is, a haven of idolatry. In March of 1523 he attacked this group again, supported even by the prior of the foundation, Justus Jonas. Although the Elector declared himself in favor of continuing endowed masses to be said, the Reformer pressed ahead once again in July. In this question the authority of God had pre-eminence over that of the Elector. As a result of the ensuing tug-of-war regarding reform of the foundation, the Elector finally forbade reform out of hand, even against the will of the foundation's directors, the majority of whom was now in favor of reform. Luther's polemics became more and more vehement. The renewed crucifixion of Christ in the canon of the mass was worse than immorality, killing, murder, theft, and adultery. It was plainly the duty of the authorities to take steps against it. In the end Frederick the Wise and the old believers of the foundation drew in their horns. On Christmas Eve of 1524 a mass purged of the worst abuses in the liturgy was celebrated. The final reform, however, was not accomplished until after the death of the Elector in 1525.

This new ordering of the church necessarily entailed also a new ordering of social and educational structures. Previously the social welfare of the poor, widows, and orphans was for the most part the responsibility of the church. These duties, as well as providing for former monks and priests, supporting poor craftsmen, and the schooling and university studies of talented children of poor parents now had to be taken over by the secular authorities, thus by city councils or regional princes.

Here too the Reformer developed important basic principles. The *Leisnig Ordinance of a Common Chest* of 1523, which Luther published with a foreword by himself, indicated the direction; the incomes and the funds of the old church are to be taken over by the secular authorities, to be administered in "common chests", and out of them the com-

*Ill. 16   Luther and the People in Dispute with the Pope and his Followers,
woodcut by Sebald Beham, ca. 1524.*

munal or regional princely social and educational obligations are to be financed. Luther furthered these beginnings
also through the formulation of a new work ethic: useful
professional work for the advantage of all is a more exalted
work of Christian charity than giving alms: "Laziness is a sin
against God's commandment, who has ordered work here.
In addition you sin against your neighbor."

From the beginning on, the Reformation also had educational implications: whoever can't read is not in a position to
understand the word of God in all its profundity. In addition the community required better educated pastors, teachers, and public officials, so that they can accomplish the
tasks arising out of the new obligations. Moreover, as a result of differing tendencies hostile to education since ca.
1522, there was a profound deterioration in education.
From 1524 on Luther therefore personally devoted himself
to the reorganization of the school system. In his writing, *To
the Councilmen of All the Cities in Germany, that They
Should Establish and Maintain Christian Schools,* he im-
plored the authorities to commit themselves to a proper education of the youth: "It therefore proper here for the council and the authorities to devote the greatest care and attention to the young … Now the prosperity of a city does not
solely derive from accumulating great treasures, raising
mighty walls and beautiful buildings, and producing many

guns and much armor … rather the best and greatest flourishing, safety and strength of a city consist in its having many fine, learned, thinking, honorable, well-brought up citizens." Everything had to be done in order to establish schools. In addition to theology in the schools, languages, history, mathematics, and music should also be taught. It was further important to provide the necessary literature in public city libraries. Children were to go to school for one or two hours a day and in addition learn a trade. Finally, in 1530, Luther brought attention again to the general obligation of attending school, in order to assure new generations of pastors, teachers, doctors and civil servants. The Reformer and his friends, above all Melanchthon, exercised direct influence on curriculum programs and the filling of positions. In Wittenberg Luther himself directed the establishment of a girls' school in 1524.

While the Reformer was thus occupied with many practical tasks, new opposition arose against him. It hit him especially hard that this came out of his own circles. Here disquiet manifested itself that the euphoric hopes of the years 1520/21, that the authorities would quickly and consistently accomplish the Reformation, were obviously a delusion. The potential for unrest was manifold and was tied to various biblical statements and Christian traditions. Many of Luther's original followers were not in a position to or willing to comprehend his teaching of the two kingdoms of God. They were of the opinion that God called for the imitation of Christ not only through the word of the gospel, but also through the immediate operation of the holy spirit. In this however, Luther thought that he discerned only a new law which he fundamentally rejected in matters of faith. In the most radical individuals such ideas were linked together with apocalyptic final days and chiliasm. By means of this they separated the "godless" from the "chosen" and therefore created the intellectual prerequisites for outrage and rebellion. All of these theological and religious postulates combined in many different ways with social dissatisfaction, as a result of which the threshold of readiness to engage in violence was dangerously lowered. Luther saw these dangers from very early on and they caused him to describe the "radical" reformers as "fanatics", "rabble rousers", and "prophets" .

A case in point was Luther's relationship with Thomas

Müntzer (Ill. 17). In 1517/18 he had belonged to the circle of Wittenberg reformers. Paradoxically, during the time of his reform activities in Jüterbog in 1519, precisely he was the first one to be described as a "Lutheran". In 1520/21, on Luther's recommendation, he worked as a preacher in Zwickau. Dismissed in the end by the town council, he tried to succeed in Bohemia with his own ideas, which he had developed in the meantime. All without success, which is the reason why he wandered around aimlessly between Nordhausen, Halle, and finally also Jena, Erfurt, and Stolberg. From Easter of 1523 to the beginning of August he finally found a position as a preacher in the electoral Saxon exclave of Allstedt.

Common to both reformers was the belief in the promises of Christ. But Müntzer came to the conclusion that a person could only receive these promises when beforehand the heart of a person were purified of all worldly endeavors, thus of seeking a life of pleasure, riches, fame, and power. Only then could God's spirit find place in the hearts of the faithful.

Such a reborn believer who had become "Christ-like" would be plainly called upon by God to fight uncompromisingly against the "godless". In his *Prince's Sermon* before

Ill. 17 Thomas Müntzer, copper engraving by Christoffel von Sichem, 1608

43

Duke John in Allstedt in July, 1524, the prophet made a final attempt to win over the temporal authorities to this view. If the princes were not to fulfill their duty to exterminate the "godless", God would snatch the sword away from them and give it to the common people. In the Peasants' War just breaking out, Müntzer saw this decision of God at last being realized.

The Peasants' War, which broke out in southern Germany in 1524, spread over also to Thuringia in April 1525. After his flight from Allstedt, Müntzer had created a center of Thuringian revolt in the free imperial city of Mühlhausen. When on the 16th of April Luther set out on a trip to Eisleben for the opening of a new school, the threatening reports reached him. Without hesitating he immediately composed his *Admonition to Peace: A Reply to the Twelve Articles*, which probably was printed as early as the beginning of May in Wittenberg. To be sure he laid the blame for the uprising on the princes and landowners, bishops, priests, and monks: "In the first place we have no one on earth to thank for this horrible insurrection except you princes and lords, especially you blind bishops and crazed priests and monks, who, still hardened of heart today, do not stop raging and ranting against the holy gospel, even though at the same time you know it is true and cannot be refuted. In addition, as temporal authorities you do nothing else but slave-drive and glory in your pomposity and haughtiness, until the poor common people are neither able to nor have any desire to stand it any longer." But he decisively rejected violent resistance and demanded an arbitration tribunal, which was to examine the requests of the peasants. When despite this the revolt broke out also in Thuringia under the leadership of Thomas Müntzer, Luther, with implacable hate, condemned the entire uprising as the work of the devil. The Reformer dared even to beard the lion in his own den, that is, in the rebellious regions. He preached in Stolberg, Wallhausen, and Nordhausen, accompanied everywhere by massive demonstrations of anger. Increasingly he stated the opinion of seeing behind the peasants the machinations of the "arch-devil" Müntzer. Now he not only justified the use of force by the princes, but clearly called for it, most decisively in his writing, *Against the Rapacious and Murdering Hordes of Peasants,* about which opinions differ even up to today. When the Thuringian peasants were defeated at the battle of Frankenhausen on May 15, with Müntzer captured and later executed, the Reformer saw in this a judgment of God against those revolting as well as the confirmation of his harsh stance. His appeal to the victors for mercy toward the vanquished met with no response (Ill. 18). Many of his followers turned away now from their former standard bearer. The Reformation had reached a parting of the ways.

Ill. 18. Military Field Tribunal, woodcut by the Petrarch-Master, ca. 1520

Father of a Family and Man of the Church (1525-1546)

Although even since 1521 many former priests and monks had entered the married state on the basis of Luther's teachings, the Reformer himself still rejected such a step for himself in autumn of 1524. During his trip to the Thuringian peasants in April 1525 he indicated for the first time his intention to marry. He wished thereby to profess his belief in his own teaching before his own feared death, and to resist the devil who goaded on the peasants. Finally at the end of May in Wittenberg his intention of wedding the runaway nun, Katherine von Bora, was rumored about. The reaction was unanimously negative: if marriage must be, then not with this one, but with another! Swift action seemed therefore to be called for. On the evening of June 13 the engagement took place in the monastery in the presence of friends. Afterwards the bridal pair was married in connection with the so-called copulation, a symbolic lying down in the marriage bed, by the Wittenberg city pastor, Luther's close friend and father confessor, Johannes Bugenhagen. Among the critics of this step was also his friend, Philipp Melanchthon, especially since he had neither been informed beforehand nor invited. In addition he was of the opinion, Katie had beguiled Luther. Nevertheless he stood up against the rumor, which had been gleefully spread by Erasmus, that both had had sexual relations before the marriage. The jurist Hieronymus Schurff opposed the marriage even more emphatically: "If this monk gets married, the whole world and the devil will laugh, and he himself will ruin everything that he has accomplished."

Katherine, born in 1499, was the daughter of an impoverished Saxon nobleman. As a nun in the Cistercian convent of Nimbschen near Grimma she was among the nine convent sisters who had fled in April of 1523 and found refuge in Wittenberg. In only a short time after her arrival she became deeply attracted to the Nuremberg patrician's son, Hieronymus Baumgärtner, who was studying in Wittenberg, and who returned her affections. The relationship, however, broke up. When finally the idea was broached of marrying her to the university rector, Kaspar Glatz, an obvious

Ill. 19 Luther and Katherine von Bora, oil on wood by Lucas Cranach the Elder (Workshop), 1528

miser and unpleasant contemporary, she hatched a small plot, probably with Luther's friend, Nikolaus von Amsdorf. In any case Amsdorf informed Luther confidentially that Katie, if it had to be that she married, would be willing to take as her husband only him, Amsdorf, or failing that, then Doctor Martin Luther. Only at this point does it seem that the Reformer's eyes were opened.

Little is known about the first weeks of marriage of the Luthers. In any case the Doctor took a break from lectures, sermons, and his correspondence. Later he expressed himself warmly about the honeymoon, which he called "kissing weeks". Yet he probably had not been an overly passionate lover. During this time he wrote to Amsdorf: " I am not on fire, but I love my spouse." Later he summarized the inner adjustment: Now he no longer sat at the table alone, and upon waking he saw a pair of pigtails lying next to him.

The Doctor of Holy Scripture did not possess riches, nor did he consider acquiring such. From 1525 on he received a salary of 200 gulden from the Elector. That was top pay at the university, which no one else but Melanchthon received. In spite of this the upkeep of his growing household devoured more means than were often available. Since, however, the Elector and his council from time to time allowed the family extra monetary payments or goods in kind,

Luther was able all his life to adhere to the principle of not demanding any fees for lectures and books. On the other hand, in 1527 he had lathe equipment sent to him from Nuremberg, in order to improve his money situation somewhat by means of his own woodworking. When it finally arrived, he made the critical, but of course ironic remark that it would not turn by itself while his assistant, Seberger, was snoring. Whether he himself ever did lathe work is questionable, in view of his probable lack of woodworking talent. Whenever Luther was too generous with his money, for example, he repeatedly assumed financial guarantees in the council for destitute Wittenbergers, Katie strove stubbornly and successfully to increase their wealth. As a result there arose differences not only between her and the Elector's chancellor, Brück, but also with her husband, who once, following a small altercation, groaned out loud: "If I ever again were to have to go courting, I would chisel myself an obedient wife out of stone." Along with brewing and selling cloister beer, Katherine busied herself especially with taking care of the garden, and thus managed, in the end always successfully, to acquire gardens and properties. The costs of these were, though, probably more than the profits brought in, because in 1532 Luther was surprised that he financially made ends meet at all. Household expenses per year amounted to 500 gulden, more than he earned. In 1535/36 he drew up an *Astonishing Accounting Between Doctor Martinus and Katie*, which reflects these problems. Slowly life returned again to the deserted cloister. Six children were born to the Luther family, of whom, however, two died as children. When in 1542 Luther's thirteen-year-old daughter, Magdalene, died in his arms, untold pain overwhelmed him. Despite the understanding that it had been God's will, a fit of crying racked him at the graveside. The motto for the upbringing of his children was that the carrot must go with the stick, whereby he brought up the boys more strictly than the girls. Like probably every father, Luther cherished high expectations for his oldest son, as a result of which he however demanded too much of him. Already at seven years of age he matriculated at the university and in 1539, thus at thirteen years of age, he earned the baccalaureate degree.

Since 1529 the six children of his probably deceased sister had also lived in Luther's household. In addition "Auntie

Lene", Katie's aunt Magdalena, who had fled from Nimb-schen convent soon after Katherine, belonged to the family. Like other professors, Luther also had students boarding and lodging in his house through which the household budget was somewhat ameliorated. Along with these, guests and refugees frequently came. Nonetheless, good-for-nothings and cheats tried to exploit their hospitality. In 1541 Luther recounted how a supposed nun had sneaked into the house under an assumed name. She was, though, the daughter of a citizen from Franconia executed in the Peasants' War. When it finally became clear that she lied, stole and was pregnant, she disappeared and tried her luck in other par-sonages. Luther was of the opinion that when practicing Christian love one must expect such incidents. Nevertheless he became from then on more cautious.

The wedding of the former monk with the former nun on June 13, 1525, at the time of the culmination of the Peasants' War, marked the final break of Luther with monasticism and clericalism, visible to the whole world, and the transition to

Ill. 20 The Luther Room in the Wittenberg Luther House

the life of a bourgeois scholar in the service of his sovereign.

Konrad Cordatus, who had fled from Hungary, was the first to begin recording Luther's Table Talks. Other table guests followed him in this. Apparently this upset Katie, which she occasionally gave vent to with cutting remarks. The writers got back at her by making comments about her supposedly domineering nature. In spite of their disputed authenticity the Table Talks are an inexhaustible source of information about Luther's personality, his life, and his work. They document in a special way the Reformer's bond with folk and life in attitude and language.

Luther enjoyed devoting what little leisure time he could to music in the home, whereby he judged his own singing talents quite self-critically. In the garden he had a bowling alley installed for his students and house guests, and his bond with nature was proverbial. In the country he meditated again and again on the wonder of creation in nature, which frequently provided him with allegories for his beliefs.

Precisely the terrible experience of the Peasants' War reinforced his view, that it was the urgent duty of the secular powers to guarantee domestic and external peace. Despite the fact that he had his whole life long so strenuously resisted the establishment of a governing church authority, he saw nevertheless, in view of actual events, no other possibility of assuring the victory of the gospel than also through sovereign measures and regulations. While the Reformer stood up in principle for allowing new structures to grow and only then to establish them, he was under pressure from his prince, who wanted to decree them immediately. What really as a matter of fact badly needed accomplishing were salary regulations for pastors and teachers. Many of them actually lived in the poorest of circumstances as a result of the collapse of the old church order. Such regulations, however, couldn't be effected without the assistance of the prince. Now it was Luther who requested help from the Elector. The fact that a portentous intervention of the state in church matters was being put forward here was justified by the professor under the concept of the right of necessity. For his part the Elector, however, at first reacted cautiously. He was still afraid that Luther was only after the state paying the pastors' and teachers' salaries. After the Imperial Diet in Speyer in 1526, which left to the territorial authorities the accomplishment of reform measures, the Reformer presented his case anew, especially since the greater part of church revenues through cloisters and foundations was turned over to the princes. The Elector's instructions regarding the visitations of June 1527 imposed broad responsibilities on the visitators: the teaching and way of life of pastors, preachers, and schoolmasters were to be examined, pastors with the old beliefs were to be settled with or pensioned, and heretics were to exiled from the land. Furthermore church revenues were to be determined, and a new ordering of salaries as well as the introduction of the divine service ordinance, worked out by Luther, were to be established. The welfare of the poor was to be assured by setting up common chests. For every district a superintendent was to be installed for the supervision of pastors. Christian morality, above all, marriage jurisdiction, were to be placed under the Elector's official staff. After a visitation had taken place in the districts of Weida and afterwards in Saalkreis in 1527, the former stronghold of Karlstadt, there finally appeared in print in March of 1528 the *Instructions for Visitators of the Pastors in Electoral Saxony*. These had been developed essentially by Melanchthon with a preface by Luther. With these the course had been set: the new order took place according to a supervisory system from above, directed by the office of the bishop, and not according to a presbyterial-synodal representation of the congregation.

Also, with the introduction of the evangelical church reorganization on Christmas 1525 in Wittenberg, the Reformer's intent was by no means a generally valid church reorganization. Rather he emphasized in his preface that in every case it was to be implemented in the spirit of Christian freedom. Yet probably already in February of 1526 the reorganization was inaugurated in the electoral patronage parishes by electoral order. Finally in June the order was given to the noble patrons to introduce this reorganization. In 1526 the church reorganization was supplemented with Luther's *German Personal Baptismal Book* with a purified liturgy, and in 1529 with his *Marriage Book*.

Even before the beginning of the Reformation one of Luther's most important concerns was to promote correct understanding among the laity of the Ten Commandments, the confession of faith, the Lord's Prayer, and of the sacraments. After Nikolaus Hausman had already suggested in the beginning of 1525 a book of instructions for children, and Luther had encouraged his co-workers in different regions toward similar undertakings, he finally made plans for his own catechism. Initially he gave catechetical sermons and called upon landlords that they force their domestics to attend them under penalty of dismissal. Out of these sermons came both of Luther's *Catechisms* in 1529, the "small one" for the laity and the "greater one" for pastors and preachers. Luther required memorization of the small catechism. If this weren't done he threatened punishment even up to exile from the country.

Ever since his earliest youth Martin had liked to sing himself. The Reformer understood music as a means of reinforcing faith, since it was capable of banishing depressing and gloomy thoughts that come from the devil. So it was no surprise that he attached great importance to German congregational hymns as a means of reinforcing faith and the Christian sense of community. A high point in Luther's work with music was the *Klug's Hymn Book*, which became a model for many subsequent hymn books (Ill. 21). In its first edition of 1529, now lost, Luther's most well-known chorale, *A Mighty Fortress is our God,* originally written in 1527, was also printed for the first time. An arrangement of the 46th psalm, it was a song of consolation for Christianity and for the once again challenged Reformer himself. For in 1527 he was again beleaguered by serious illness and spiritual depression. In Wittenberg the plague broke out. In Bavaria a follower of Luther, Leonard Kaiser, paid the price

Ill. 21 Klug's Hymn Book, Wittenberg 1533

of being a witness for the Reformation with his blood.

Although it became clear, especially in his sermons, that the professor "listened to the way the ordinary person spoke", that is, preached in popular speech, he did not necessarily agree with them. If he felt it called for, and that was not seldom the case, he could properly read his Wittenberg community the Riot Act. Above all, irregular attendance at divine service and an un-Christian life style again and again provoked harsh criticism from him. He included all sectors of life in his sermons. Frequently he expressed his thoughts without a manuscript before the community, before noble men and in his own house. Veit Dietrich wrote down the sermons given in the family, through which the so-called *House Postil* came into being. For Luther the sermon was the center of divine service and thus the decisive means of strengthening Christian faith.

In addition to that, Luther devoted special attention to the continuing translation of the Bible from the original languages into German. After the first part of Luther's translation of the Old Testament had appeared already in 1523, the translation of the remaining parts was drawn out over many years, since Luther was interrupted repeatedly during this important work by daily events, organizational tasks, and by illness. After he was finally able to make decisive progress with the translation of the Prophetic Books at Fortress Coburg in 1530, the first complete Lutheran Bible, Old and New Testaments in one volume, finally appeared in 1534 (Ill. 22). The Lutheran Bible translation quickly became the most read and most purchased book of the 16th century. Even representatives of the Roman church saw themselves now forced to translate the bible into the vernacular languages. Since in doing so they relied upon Luther's translation, in the end they too contributed to the spread of the Lutheran Bible.

The time up to 1532 was politically very unstable. In both great confessional camps there were again and again efforts to forge political-military alliances. At first however the Imperial Diet in Speyer from June to August 1526 defused the situation again. The compromise left reform measures to the discretion of the princes. As a result an imperial law basis was above all created for the reorganization of the evangelical church. When in 1528 landgrave Philip of Hesse, as a result of fictitious rumors about an impending

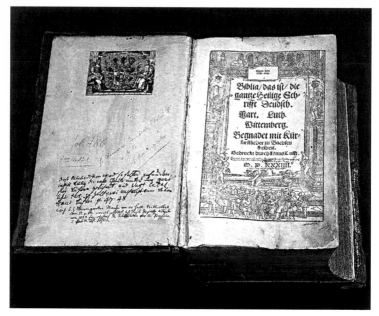

Ill. 22 The First Complete Lutheran Bible, Wittenberg, 1534

military action by the old believers (Pack Affair), contemplated a preventive war, Luther emphatically rejected it, even threatened his departure from electoral Saxony. Luther's and Melanchthon's firm stand impressed Elector John, and the plan was rejected. The Imperial Diet in Speyer of 1529, against whose anti-reform recess decree the reform estates drew up a protest (thereafter people also called them Protestants), exacerbated the situation again. But it was then defused by the offer of the Emperor to negotiate also the religious question during the Imperial Diet scheduled for 1530 in Augsburg. Behind this readiness of the Emperor to compromise stood the acute threat to the empire by the Turks; repulsing them required also the support of the Protestants. The electoral Saxon delegation to the imperial diet, which was under the leadership of the Elector himself, included, in addition to his councilors, also Lutheran theologians, especially Melanchthon. Luther himself had to remain behind in Fortress Coburg since he was still under the ban. Here he spent 156 days. With letters and printed exhortations he tried to encourage his friends in Augsburg. At the same time the Reformer himself was mired in a different situation.   Illness, loneliness, and the forced inactivity strained his nerves. On top of this came the sad news of the death of his father. In spite of that, or perhaps precisely because of that, the Reformer summoned the strength from his faith, to help his despairing friends in Wittenberg with letters to get through their deep depressions.

Although the Lutheran imperial estates were able on June 25, 1530 to read out the Lutheran confessional writing, the Augsburg Confession, which had been worked out by Melanchthon, and which in itself represented de facto a considerable success in terms of recognition, all compromise negotiations came to nothing. The imperial diet's recess decree was severely anti-reform and forbade any future innovations. The final imperial diet decree even demanded the restoration of the old conditions. For this the Emperor issued an ultimatum of April 15, 1531. In the event of non-compliance military measures were threatened. The logical consequence of this was the founding of the Smalcald League, a defense alliance of the evangelical imperial estates. In the end, after intensive negotiations and also vehement intra-Protestant debates, a peace was agreed upon at the Nuremberg Imperial Diet on July 23, 1532. It largely confirmed the confessional status quo and thus for the time being assured external peace. Thus the Reformation could spread peacefully. In 1539 the Duchy of Saxony changed over to the Lutheran confession. In 1541 electoral Brandenburg followed suit.   These developments nevertheless caused the political-confessional parity situation in the empire to begin tottering again and ultimately led to the catastrophe of the Smalcald War, which was to break out directly after Luther's death.

Old and New Enemies (1525-1546)

Luther's efforts after 1525 to advance the Reformation under the conditions of secure princely rule were during his whole life subjected to attacks from the most varied, indeed conflicting sides. Many a former follower accused him of having betrayed the peasants and made peace with the ruling circles. The adherents of Rome still held Luther, as the supposed spiritual father of the rebellion, responsible for the bloodbath. Such attacks and others compelled the Reformer again and again to pick up the gauntlet and to stand up for his ideas and to put them in concrete terms. Tenaciously and unwaveringly the "sworn Doctor of the Holy Scripture" defended his teaching with weapons which ranged from the most polished theological argumentation through irony and biting ridicule up to the most ranting insults.

A significant opponent of Luther arose in the person of Erasmus of Rotterdam. The power of the people's movement, which caused the unity of Christianity, Europe, and the sciences invoked by many Humanists to appear to be an illusion, led to many a Humanist turning away from the Reformation. Symptomatic of this development was the dispute between Erasmus and Luther over the freedom of the will. Both had early on recognized the incompatibility of their positions. Already in 1517 Luther's criticism was that in Erasmus' world-view the human was superior to the divine. Two years later Erasmus established the non-Humanistic in Luther, who as early as 1518 in the Heidelberg disputation had rejected the capability of a person only even to will the good by one's own efforts. In 1524 the battle broke out into the open. With his tract *De libero arbitrio* (On Free Will), Erasmus flung down the gauntlet, which Luther picked up, and in 1526 hurled it back with *De servo arbitrio* (The Bondage of the Will). Erasmus ascribed a certain efficacy to the free will of a person toward the good, acting together with divine grace. However much these views seem to correspond more with thinking today, Erasmus thus ultimately adopted in those days the theoretical positions of the old church.

Since 1525 a vehement controversy had flared up in the reform camp over the sacrament of the Lord's supper, at first between Luther and Karlstadt, later between the Luther and Zwingli. While the Swiss reformers regarded the Lord's supper more as a memorial supper service for strengthening faith, Luther claimed, on the basis of the omnipotence of God, that the body and blood of Christ were actually present in, with, and under the bread and wine of the Lord's supper. This opposition put a strain on a coordinated position of adherents of the Reformation vis-à-vis imperial politics. For this reason the Protestant imperial estates, above all landgrave Philip of Hesse, made an effort to settle the controversy. To this end the landgrave invited Luther, Melanchthon, Zwingli, Oecolampadius, Bucer, Brentz, and other reformers in 1529 to the Marburg religious colloquy (Ill. 23). Although after hard duels of words a tortuous formula of understanding was reached in the *Marburg Articles,* the fundamental differences of opinion could not be resolved. The *Wittenberg Concord* of 1536, which formulated a unified view of the Lord's supper question reached between Wittenbergers and southern German reformers, did not include the Swiss reformers - the relationship with them even hardened again.

The Anabaptist movement had had its origin in the peasant and plebeian opposition in Zurich since 1523. While

Ill. 23 Marburg Religious Colloquy, colored woodcut, 1557

Zwingli put the accomplishing of the Reformation in the hands of the council, his critics wanted to build the new church completely independent of secular power. Their symbol became adult or faith baptism. After the quelling of the Peasants' War the Anabaptist movement became a gathering point of forces in opposition to the reform movement. Alongside unity in certain matters (for example, rejection of any spiritual or secular authority in questions of faith or communal life, refusal of oaths) sharply differing views existed within the movement. The thinking and feelings of the Anabaptists varied on the one hand between resignation in the form of quietist acquiescence in fate and spiritualized piety, as well as on the other hand chiliastic end of the world expectations, apocalyptic visions and secret insurrection plans. From the very beginning the Anabaptists were persecuted and cruelly punished. As a result of a wave of persecutions in 1528/1529 the strength of the southern German Anabaptists broke, and the center of the movement repositioned itself to northern Germany. The high point was reached in the Anabaptist Kingdom in Münster. In 1534/1535 militant Anabaptists attempted to found there the "New Jerusalem" and thus the dreamed of kingdom of equality. Property ownership conditions were transformed according to the apostolic ideal of common ownership. Gold, silver, and money had to be surrendered, food reserves were catalogued, and seven delegates administered together these goods. As a result of the siege conditions imposed on the city by the army of the bishop of Münster, draconian laws were promulgated and characteristics of sectarianism increased (temporary introduction of polygamy). In the night of the 25th to the 26th of June 1535 the defenders, weakened by hunger, could no longer withstand the superior forces. A gruesome military court and butchering of those defeated ensued.

Since the Anabaptists in electoral Saxony never had any significant influence, they played only a minor role in Luther's polemics. At first he rejected to be sure their teachings, but condemned the reprisals taken against them. After the suppression of the Münster Anabaptist Kingdom however, the Wittenberg reformers, especially Melanchthon, condemned the Anabaptists with harsh words similar to those used earlier with the revolting peasants.

From 1537 on, renewed opposition arose out of the innermost circles. One of the earliest supporters of the Reformation, Johann Agricola, also called "Master Eisleben" after the town of his birth, began to advocate biased ideas about the relationship of law (the totality of moral standards of the Old Testament, in particular the Ten Commandments) to the gospel. Luther was always fundamentally of the conviction that the law as a prerequisite for the recognition of sin and thus also for the forgiveness of sin, as promised in the gospel, exercises an important function for Christians. On the other hand Agricola now taught that the law had no significance at all for the faith and life of Christians, and that Luther betrayed his own teaching if he now professed something else. Theses, counter theses, disputations as well as mediation attempts by Melanchthon in the end accomplished only that the differences became more sharply delineated. Finally Luther concluded that he was forced to see in Agricola, as already previously in Müntzer and the Swiss, a tool of the devil. Having come under ever-increasing pressure, Agricola at last secretly left Wittenberg in August of 1540, in order to become the court preacher in Berlin for Electoral Brandenburg.

In the hate-filled attitude of the aging Reformer toward Jews there is nothing to gloss over or to excuse, even though one naturally should not lose sight of the background. Since about 1540 Luther had become increasingly convinced of living in the actual final times. Whoever in Luther's view closed their eyes to the gospel, such as old believers, heretics, Turks, and yes, even Jews too, with those now any understanding or compromise were once and for all out of the question. In the tract *On the Jews and Their Lies* from the year 1543, particularly in the third part, the Reformer fell back into the traditional anti-Semitic prejudices of Christianity. He dashed his own promising beginnings in his writing which appeared in 1523, *That Jesus Christ was Born a Jew*, and thus had an influence, without doubt unintentionally, on the fact that later, even in Protestantism, anti-Semitic prejudices could establish themselves.

Up to the end of his life Luther continued his struggle against Rome. Again and again there was cause for this, for example in 1528 a mandate of the bishop of Meissen against the chalice for the laity, the intensified actions against the Reformation in different old belief areas at the beginning of the 1530's, as well as the constant attempts of Duke George to carry on controversy and take action against the Reformation. Nonetheless these more regional clashes took place under the conditions of a relative balance of power between Protestants and old believers in the Empire. The curia tried with every means to win back power and influence in the Holy Roman Empire of the German Nation. The main focus of the fundamental arguments became the question of the summoning of a council. In 1524, after the Emperor had forbidden the German National Council demanded by Luther and the estates in opposition, he then endeavored to prepare a general council in the interest of his universalist plans. But opposing political interests of the European powers, changing alliances, and continuing war turmoil prevented this. Luther spoke out decisively against all attempts to hold the council under the control of the curia. The council that was finally convened in Trent (1545 till 1563) took place nevertheless under the control of the pope and therefore without the participation of the Protestants. It renewed the theology and form of the Roman church fundamentally and shaped it until the Second Vatican Council in the 20th century.

Old Age and Death - Legacy

The older Luther became, the more he was compelled to relive the experience of all those who with noble intentions have begun something of greatness, that its realization in the "lowly spheres" of daily life is far more complicated than originally expected. Again and again he well-nigh despaired over the fact that the preaching of the gospel bore too little fruit in the life of the congregation. Increasing immorality and inadequate appreciation of the church's blessings, of the divine service, and of the sacraments were frequently condemned by him in his sermons and caused him, the longer they went on, the more to come to the conviction that the final judgment day would soon bring this earthly vale of tears to an end. After a trip to Zeitz in 1545 he finally didn't want to return to Wittenberg any more. "My heart has grown cold, so much so that I don't like being there any more." Katie should sell everything and go with him to the farm in Zulsdorf. He would rather eat begged-for bread than martyr himself in his last days with the "disorderly goings-on" in Wittenberg. In the end, however, his friends were still able to prevail upon him to go back.

Despite or perhaps because of such disappointments Luther remained tirelessly active right up to the end of his life. The most important thing was to resist the devil to the very end. When in March of 1545 the fable of his supposed death - originating in Italy - reached him, he appropriated it, plainly amused, and had it printed in Wittenberg with a postscript, as the product of a "poor, miserable, sorry specimen of a priest". In his concluding remark he declared sarcastically that as far as this type of hate from his enemies was concerned it didn't bother him in the least.

The Reformer made his last journey on earth to his birthplace, Eisleben. His connection with his relations and with the Mansfeld count's house had never broken off. The attempts of count Albert to induce the smelter owners to sell their smelters by means of exorbitant increases in the hereditary leases, which also directly threatened Luther's brother Jakob and his son-in-law, encountered determined criticism from the Reformer. In spite of that, his authority, of all things, was now supposed to help resolve inheritance disputes and other strife within the count's family. For this reason, after a last sermon in Wittenberg on January 17, 1546, Luther set out for Mansfeld in the company of his three sons. Only after three days of waiting could the company of travelers cross the Saale, which was swollen with ice and floodwaters. Despite a fainting spell later in the trip, he didn't allow himself to be deterred from preaching another four times during the first half of February. Tired of life he nevertheless declared two days before his death: "When I get home again in Wittenberg, I'll lie down immediately in my casket and give the maggots a fat doctor to nibble on." Notwithstanding this, he mobilized all his energy to be able to conclude the arduous and difficult negotiations successfully. On February 16 he was granted a first success with two important agreements.

In the night of the 17th over the 18th of February, 1546 Luther died in his birthplace of Eisleben in his 63rd year of life. At the order of the Elector his body was transferred to Wittenberg and, with great numbers of the Wittenbergers in attendance, was buried there in the castle church on February 22.

The last written words of Luther, put down on paper two

Ill. 24 Funeral Sermon for Luther, colored woodcut, 1557

days before his death, bring home to us wisely and poetical-
ly, indeed almost like a legacy, both the greatness as well as
the nothingness of human existence. They testify to the un-
broken confidence of the Reformer in his faith, also or precisely in the face of death: "No one can understand the pas-
toral poetry of Virgil unless he has been a shepherd for five
years. No one can understand Virgil's poems about farming,
unless he had been a husbandman for five years. The letters
of Cicero can't be understood by anyone, unless he has
lived in a great metropolis for 25 years. No one may claim to
have sufficiently savored holy scripture, unless he has led
the congregations with prophets, such as Elijah and Elisa,
John the Baptist, Christ, and the apostles. Do not attempt
this divine Aeneid, but rather bow down deeply worship-
ping before their footprints! We are beggars, that is true!"

i Wittenberg information

WELCOME TO
LUTHERSTADT WITTENBERG!

"... discover world history"

The members of Wittenberg-Information are pleased to assist you.

We can offer you:

- City tours by our qualified guides
- Museum and church visits
- Individual arrangements of full or half day programs
- Hotel and private accommodations
- Hotel booking service for groups
- Restaurant facilities
- Sale of souveniers

We are looking forward to you visit.

Our address
FREMDENVERKEHRSBÜRO
WITTENBERG-INFORMATION

Schlossplatz 2
06886 Lutherstadt Wittenberg

Telephone	01149-3491-49 86 10	
Fax	01149-3491-49 86 11	
	accomodation service	
Telephone	01149-3491-41 48 48	*daily open*
Internet Address	www.wittenberg.de	
e-mail	wb_info@wittenberg.de	

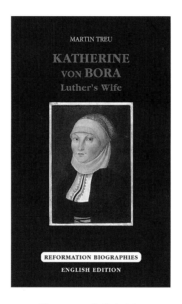